**Falco Tarassaco**

# Learning
## *to* Die

DAMANHUR

LEARNING TO DIE
di Falco Tarassaco (Oberto Airaudi)

First italian edition: Imparare a morire, 1978

The poems that appear in this book are taken from
"Poems of my Sixteenth Years", by Oberto Airaudi,
published by Appiano, Turin, 1967.

Translation: Elaine Baxendale
Graphic design: Albatros Finferlo

ISBN: 9788890863769

Devodama srl, Vidracco (TO), Italy
COPYRIGHT 2015© by FRANCA NANI

Cover: Selfic painting by Oberto Airaudi May 9-18, 2000.

# Introduction

*"Learning to Die" is a discourse about life and death. Falco Tarassaco, Oberto Airaudi, published it in 1978. It was his first book after founding Damanhur.*

*This is a book of hope. The hope that our life is always full, dignified and meaningful. The hope that we can be fully aware of who we really are as human and spiritual beings.*

*In this book, Falco shows us a way not to be afraid of death. The experiences, the meditations, the suggestions contained in this text speak of a simple truth: death is a part of life, and it is one of our spiritual tasks to learn to accept it. We must know how it happens, so that we can die well and help our loved ones in dying.*

*Beyond life there is death, which is still life, says Falco. To speak of death is to speak of life. We start moving closer to death from the moment in which we are born. From one transition to another. Childhood and then adolescence help us to prepare for autonomy, adulthood and "real life." But at what stage of life, do we prepare for death?*

*Who teaches us how to die?*

*Death must be addressed as we live. It should be regarded as an important element of our existence during the time when we do not yet have direct links with it; when we are young and healthy; when we are not grieving the loss of a loved one. We just need to accept the most self-evident truths about life: everything with a beginning also has an end, and the end is certainly no less important than the beginning!*

Normally, we do not enjoy considering the proximity of death, the sense of the unknown, the detachment from our body, from our things, and the loss of our loved ones. Falco simply suggests not to exclude the thought of death, not to deny its presence, and then trust our inner guidance in our encounter with it. Indeed, together with love, hope, hunger and curiosity, death is a companion in our lives. Falco seems to suggest that we should leave it a half-open door, so when the time comes, we can pass through it and embrace it without fear and confusion.

Falco presented this book forty years ago, a long time if we consider the average lifespan of a book today. A short time if we ponder the magnitude of the theme. He offers thoughts and reflections that can help us stop fearing that fateful and unavoidable moment, both for our loved ones and ourselves.

How? By reflecting on "Learning to Die," as Falco suggests. You will not find in this book an indepth treatment of the phenomenology of death —accident, suicide, euthanasia and then the burial or cremation—not because they are unimportant, but because what matters most is the serenity and recovery of the dignity that accompanies death and therefore accompanies life. What you will find, then, are practical suggestions, methods and directions on how to prepare for dying with awareness and harmony, and how to assist and comfort your loved ones during, and right after, their passage.

*Stambecco Pesco*

# Learning
## *to* Die

# Why this talk about death

If you are wondering why this talk about death, I can tell you that we are all interested in death, given that we all must die. All of us, moreover, are afraid of it. Whether we like it or not, every one has their own time marked out, as if, the moment they are born, there is written in a book the day and hour when they will die[1].

Death is the only constant in all our incarnations: every time we die we have a new experience, different from before, totally unique.

In the West, we are afraid of death, we are afraid of losing our individuality, of no longer being ourselves, of no longer being able to say: "Me!"

1. In the vision of Falco, time is articulated into infinite ramifications, each containing all possible events, including different hypotheses about our date of death. As a result, there is no single fatal predestination, but the possibility of orienting events, in a field of possibilities already foreseen. The theories on the laws that govern the universe and the ramifications of time are illustrated in the volume "Spiritual Physics," by Coyote Cardo, Damanhur School of Meditation Press, printed for private use, 2014.

In the East, however, death is generally looked upon as part of a broader picture, where every being, as a unique being, must disappear because as long as there is some part of an ego, as long as it survives, there can be no advancement in the Great Tree of Humanity.

Thus, this is meant to be a discussion that allows you to prepare yourself for a moment in life you will certainly have to face.

Personally, I believe in reincarnation, also because I remember my past lives; however this is a personal conviction, and I do not intend to influence anyone. I write these notes not to persuade, but to give my small contribution to understanding a very important subject; paradoxically the most important one in our whole life. We live to learn how to die.

I remember, together with my lives, also my deaths, often not very pleasant ones, and I would like others to avoid repeating the mistakes I have made in the past.

I do not know if remembering, in this case, is a good thing or not, but if I have been allowed to in order to share it with others, I accept this task.

Whoever reads this has their own religious beliefs, and I have no intention of questioning them. I am not interested in anyone's religion in this sense, nor in the way others look at death. I wish to give some advice, each person may decide whether to follow it or not; I wish to leave within whoever reads this a trace that I feel might be of use. With this work, albeit rather limited, I intend simply to pass on technical notes and practical advice. I realize I am presenting a rather surprising view of the problem... but this is my experience.

13

Learning to live is not easy, as we all know: we have to manage to "let ourselves live."

That does not mean not acting, but rather welcoming every event as something natural, and not worrying too much. We must learn not to be slaves to money, to clothes and so on; we must also know how to manage our attachments, without hanging on anxiously to them.

We must, in the end, be fully present with all of ourselves in every moment of our earthly existence, or rather, live in the now.

Think about it! Begin to feel yourself being: you are born in this precise moment!

Death, a word with a strange feel, that evokes fear in some, amazement in others, emptiness, memories of people we knew when they were alive, and then lost to its ivory whiteness.

Do you remember? As small children, when an old person left us, we were amazed we did not feel so much grief and we tried hard to cry like the others, whose eyes were swollen and red, fearing someone would accuse us of being bad, because we did not feel anything...

Perhaps, in our childish minds, we felt it was not true that grandfather was dead, in the sense of being gone forever, rather that he had only moved house. Wisdom?

The naivety of little children often hides so much of it...
Vaguely, we felt that grandfather, whenever we needed
him, would come and help us, comfort us, support us for
the rest of our life.

If we all had remained psychic or had become so by
cultivating that talent, we could help others to die,
to leave, to shuffle off the cobwebs of the body, to leave
the cocoon...

If then, as children, we were distanced from our intuition
and, perhaps, made fun of, now we can relearn those
things. I am referring to out-of-body experiences, death,
planes of existance and the bodies of the human being[2].

Let's learn to die: then we will know how to live well!

2. In addition to the physical body, each human being is made of surrounding
energy bodies. These energy bodies, which have a specific vibration, a certain
frequency, allow us to communicate with other kinds of beings and to
participate in different planes of reality. Out-of-body experience, for instance, is
a phenomenon that happens when one of these bodies, the astral body, leaves
the physical body, sometimes voluntarily, often during sleep.

There is a noticeable pinch of humor in death. Isn't it rather funny to push oneself for years, days and minutes to assert one's own personality, to acquire worth, to attain importance and then, as it gets good... to die like the last of the worms? And in just the same manner, also the conviction, almost believable, of the immortality of one's own cause?

It is not by conserving your body for a long time that you will become eternal; it is only a garment and you cannot identify with a garment. You are not your clothing. I would like to paraphrase the old saying, my way: "It's the habit that makes the monk."

So many other things can also make a human being, according to the intelligence and the beliefs of each: money, power, etc. To be more precise, I would like to say: "It is man who makes man; it is death that makes man, it is love that makes man; it is humor, in the end, that makes man!"

It is said that God, the Great Joker, made the human being in his/her own image and likeness. A most amusing idea...! Well then, when we laugh heartily at something about which we intuit the divinely funny side, now in that moment we please the Divinity.

When we get ill, we tend to think about things that, normally, we overlook. Being a little more alone with ourselves, all those masks, that we put on to look better in front of others, fall apart, disintegrate and drop away from our face. As never before, we take note of the details of our body; we notice, for the first time, an organ only because it is sick and we discover that the pain, which we thought was unbearable, is only a detail of the illness.

Often the body and the spirit become sick together, since diseases have a correspondence in the subtle bodies. When we become ill, we must get used to thinking of the suffering body as something separate from ourselves.

Death has a very precise feel, made up of letting go, indifference, apprehension, and nostalgia. Sometimes, regret at not having lived enough is added to the cocktail with a dash of hope. The important thing is to prepare oneself within. To walk with death! It is like the child-bride awaiting, with both fear and desire, the first wedding night: she does not know exactly what to expect, but she yearns to find out... Death fascinates, attracts and repulses, all at the same time.

When it is time—and we will sense it—we should let it take over, let it cradle us with its sweetness. Let's sink into it gently, just like a baby in its mother's womb, surrounded by the warm, safe amniotic fluid.

In the state between sleep and wakefulness, at times, it happens that we can scarcely feel our body. In such a moment... we could really let ourselves go, instead of deciding, having thought about it for a moment: "But no, not yet, not this time. No!" And then we make contact with our body again.

But the fact of deciding, in that moment, whether to live or to let ourselves die, and to then savor that decision, leads us to observe the deeds and events of the following day with greater responsibility, because they represent the fruit of free choice...

We can kill in so many ways, but the most common weapon is indifference. We can fight this crime by learning to think not only of ourselves, in an egotistical manner, but also of others a little more. Often someone says to me: "I who have never harmed a fly, I am treated so bad; everyone hates me and speaks ill of me!" It is always the others, who are the bad ones. And yet, we know: the truth is always somewhere in between, all the good is not on one side and the bad on the other.

Preparing to die also means not leaving harsh words behind. Never wish someone dead because, in reality, doing so you wish their being killed along with suffering and not a good death. Only a few esoteric practitioners, in touch with the Mysteries of life and death, are in the habit of wishing each other a Good Death.

Each of us wonders: "Why do we live? Why do we die? What law rules the existence of humankind?" If, while crossing a field, we trip up and inadvertently tread on an ant hill, the lives of hundreds of ants will be suddenly upset by mere carelessness. Are they aware of this fact? Of course not.

As a causative agent, we are beyond anything they can comprehend: they can neither see us, nor imagine us, they can't even fathom that a creature like uscould exist in their world. Thus they will attribute the disastrous event to a thousand other causes, but certainly not to our unsteady step.

In the same way, God is something completely beyond what our intelligence can understand and explain, belonging to another dimension altogether. To wish to understand the designs of God, to attribute behavior or intention, is an act of pride, and also of ignorance. If we could really explain all these things, we would already be with God[3].

It is important to note the respect that we must give to life and death is not limited just to human beings, but includes animals as well. Thus, we must respect also the death of animals. If we amuse ourselves by causing the death of animals, it is certain, in accord with cosmic laws, that what we have done to them will come back to us.

To practice vivisection or torture animals—out of a more or less admitted bent for sadism, more or less hidden behind scientific purposes—is something horrible and absurd. We shall find ourselves in the same situation, from every point of view, because by putting them to a certain type of death, we accumulate so much of that same death in our thoughts, that we precipitate it upon ourselves.

21

3. The universe in which we live, in the teachings of Falco, is pervaded by a divine energy that participates in the existence of any form. Life is a path through which, experience after experience, we enter into contact with the part of Divinity that dwells within us, in order to reunite with the comprehensive divine essence of the universe.

## ME I.

*I am like so many others,*
*and different from everyone.*
*I live in my portion*
*of the infinite moment.*
*I exist and I think.*
*I try like everyone to survive.*
*I search for an ideal to live for.*
*I have found in myself an ideal to defend*
*and I shall hold on till the end.*

Each of us exists simultaneously not only in human form, but also as an animal and a plant[4], because we need those kind of experiences too; and it is thus doubly absurd and incomprehensible to act with cruelty towards another "oneself."

An animal can sense when it is the moment of its death; if we paid a minimum of attention, we too would sense it normally. But, usually, these days, we do everything to hide from it. For an animal, to prepare for death means collecting itself and finding what might be its inner space. It hides to take refuge a little while, so that it can die with a certain dignity.

There is always respect for the death of another animal, at least among evolved animals; even on the part of vultures or other predators, which could

4. The human soul is not bound to the physical human form in which, normally, we are present. We are a much vaster, more universal being. In this sentence Falco refers to our divine part, that living, intelligent spirit, that descends into physical bodies, inhabits them and evolves-through experiences in various forms within the physical world.

perfectly well attack to feed but, instead, they wait. I do not remember ever having seen an animal attack another that is dying; they wait, rather, for it to die, even when it is no longer capable of defending itself—with the sole exception of insects.

Indeed, the other animals remain close to the sick animal, until it is dead, to give it a bit of warmth and comfort. Only an animal that is suffering and has no possibility of surviving is deliberately killed by another, precisely to put an end to its suffering.

Humans do not distinguish themselves from animals for their intelligence, but for their imagination. Or rather, they should distinguish themself for their imagination. A dog can grasp the commands of his master, but the latter has absolutely no idea what his faithful friend means to tell him when he barks. Thus, should not the more intelligent of the two be the one who understands?

It is useless being proud of being part of the human race only because a few individuals have come up with great inventions. What value does it have? How do we prove our own creativity if we spend our entire lives simply making use of what others have invented?

I am not saying that we all must become inventors, but creators, yes!

But instead of inventing life in the many beautiful forms of their imagination, every-day humans conceive systems that take us closer to death; a death that is the fruit of our own egoism and our own stupidity.

The stressful life in so many work places is mental torture, constant and unending. Breathing exhaust fumes from cars, stuffing oneself with pills, bathing in the polluted sea, eating junk food and drinking artificial coloring: this is a lack of respect for our bodies, and is simply torture on a vast scale. It is taking death day by day. And it is no excuse saying it is always the fault of others, in order to avoid our own responsibility, if only because—we said it before—it is not true that it is all someone else's fault.

We could also look at all this as self-punishment on an unconscious level for having spoiled our environment. Humanity judges and punishes itself. Psychology recognizes similar reasoning.

If humankind persists, with all these systems, in wanting to destroy itself, it is because something isn't working in society. Every society has the type of death it deserves; perhaps induced by a chemical formula. If we cause our deaths in so many different ways, it is because we really deserve it.

Look at history: those peoples who had recourse to violence, generally, were destroyed by war, as a natural consequence of the violence they manifested. Thus, today, in the time of consumerism, there is a tendency towards suicide with an overdose of pills, food, etc. Cancer, in this age, is an illness typical of excess; it has always to do with excess: colorings, x-rays, fear, and so on.

Thus, today, we too are deciding what our death, the end of our society, will be.

I refute this type of society and I am trying to move beyond it by creating a new city with some brothers and sisters, called Damanhur.

For there can be new ways of living, and also of dying, and new relationships—or rather, much older ones—with nature.

Who remembers that phrase from the French students of May 1968, "Power to the imagination?" We must live with our imagination. Rather than dying day by day for fear of being late at the office, rather than giving myself a heart attack when the alarm goes off, or having an accident on the production line, I prefer dropping dead from exhaustion in the fields, while I'm hoeing my beans. And to die in the sun, in the open air, looking at the greenery of the plants, and to be able to say,

"At last my time has come... soon I shall be under the ground with my beans... In fact, I will help them grow as I've always done."

But it is just as well certain bodies do not end up in the earth, they would pollute it! Better to put them in the mortuary and embalm them... even if they are no longer good for anything because they are full of rubbish.

Respect for life is extended to plants too, of course. Given the opportunity to save a plant, let's do so. Thus, upon the birth of a child, it is a beautiful tradition to plant a tree; they can grow together like playmates, and help each other. The two of them will settle into a very special, direct relationship, tuning in together. They might even get sick at the same time, or have a crisis in the same period; but they will manage to help each other.

And you who are reading this, even if you do not share my ideas on reincarnation, on the awareness of trees and of all other living beings, try however to utilize your imagination, in order to live in a more lively manner. Remember that imagination creates the power of humankind; try to be one of those who are creating new things, not one of the masses who keep on, for the whole of their lives, doing the same things.

It is worth living only if you "risk" using your own imagination, to avoid forever being conditioned.

30

It is convenient if an individual always behaves in a predictable way: it is easier for any form of power to control him.

And they who have worked loyally for thirty-five years, without being absent once, will receive an awful tin medal. Even so, they will save themselves if all those years, they have lived with consciousness moment to moment. On the other hand, if they have always lived for tomorrow, forever tomorrow, when they retire they will no longer know what to do, and will have only wasted time. In other words, life itself.

Among the plant life on our planet there are also numerous nature spirits, which we, for our convenience, have anthropomorphized, identifying them, for example, with the fairies and the gnomes. One of them is the god Pan, who in antiquity was the personification of nature, and was then identified by Christianity as the devil. They could not have done him a greater disservice!

Nature spirits are no longer happy to live in a world like this, where at times we destroy everything to the last bush; hence they do not love humans, who are driving them away.

They are patient but the time will come when they will punish us. The creation of new bacteria can in fact be interpreted as nature's response to our behavior. From 1945 until today, bacteria have progressed approximately a million years with respect to humankind.

We have modifed them so much with the use of penicillin, that today we are forced to create ever new antibiotics to try to control them. Thus, while before one drug was enough, today we need hundreds. And we call this "progress..."

Humanity is very childish in its practical applications, because it does not see sufficiently clearly the consequences of what it does. We are like a child trying to shove a piece of wire into an electric socket to see what happens, until it gets a shock. A child, however, lives with a great deal of imagination, while man, who should be responsible and figure out the consequences of his own actions, does not make use even of that, and thus does not have the means of the child.

Look at people when they go camping: almost always they leave plastic bags and empty tins around, so that the surrounding fields cannot be cultivated any more; they will become polluted and all this will end up, in the long run, coming back to them.

The same thing goes, for example, regarding the use of DDT[5], used against insects and then found in the penguins at the South Pole, which accumulates, ultimately, in the human liver.

Similarly, the gas from aerosol sprays in the atmosphere is seriously damaging the ozone layer, and we are experiencing the consequences. And every time, going to buy a newspaper, we start the car engine, we do something similarly detrimental.

This lack of responsibility is part of a collective death wish; it is a sentence that humanity has pronounced on itself.

But who is willing to give up their creature comforts? The fear of death, and above all of the pain connected with death, results in human beings looking for a worse death all the time.

5. Bearing in mind the first edition of this book was in 1978: today we should say atrazine, rather than DDT, but the essence of the matter does not change.

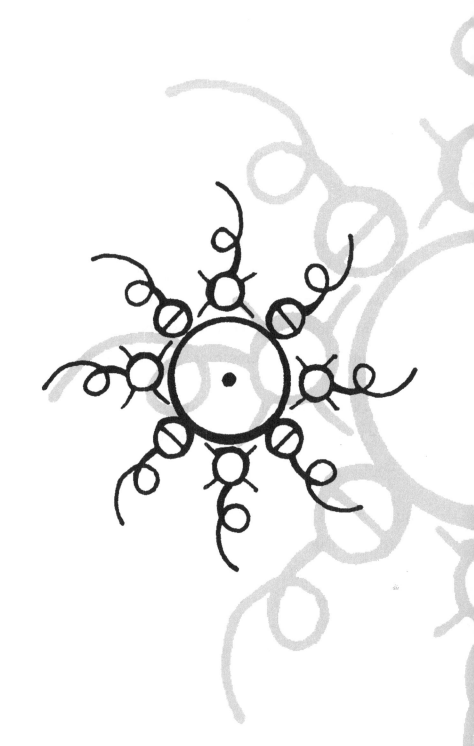

# THE SURVIVOR

*I keep on walking*
*my lonely life*
*while every now and then*
*some old man stops*
*and falls asleep in the grass.*
*With every step I too draw*
*ever closer to my patch of green,*
*ready waiting*
*and all around me*
*they keep on falling,*
*falling down,*
*falling down*
*the people who*
*walked with me.*

Think of the excessive amount of penicillin and vaccinations: rather than strengthening the body's resistance, they make the bacteria more resistant and make them multiply.

Clearly whoever chooses to take a pill every time they have a headache, should not be surprised if they get a bad toxic reaction. And as even conventional medicine well knows, the toxicity is noticeable only the first time.

36   I know several young people who are afraid of death; youngsters around eighteen/twenty years of age who have a genuine terror of it, even just to hear it talked about. Someone put this fear into them, somehow. It's one thing to be afraid of war, which is decidedly ugly, and another to be afraid of death in general.

But this fear, in some cases, is like wanting to do away with oneself; it is almost looking for death. Indeed, when you have a holy fear of it, you are often drawn to death as if it were a magnet.

One of the stupidest deaths is that of a high-speed car crash, speeding above the limit, simply for the risk of it. Throughout history, humans have always had to face risks: the challenge of nature, the dangers of the hunt, physical effort itself. Now that all this is no more, there remains inside us the deep felt need to exceed, somehow, our quota of risk which, unfortunately, we live out in the most stupid of ways.

As in the case I have just talked about: it's one thing to die in an accident that is not your fault, it's another thing to put at risk the lives of others. That denotes contempt for values, contempt for life, looking for suicide: it is one of the many frustrations humanity has felt, ever since we lost our connection with the right way to live.

Even animals do away with themselves, but for much more noble reasons. For a while around here, so many animals have been getting run over and killed on the roads. It is not by accident: it is a case of suicide.

When animals—for the most part dogs and cats—choose this type of death, it is a sign of the times. This age is no longer suitable for them, and they feel they cannot cope with it, because conditions for a harmonious life have changed, contact with the environment is lacking, and even humanity—above all humanity!—has changed profoundly.

Moreover, for so many animals, death is forced upon them by pollution. Think of the birds, of the gulls who fly above the sea. Because of a tanker that has lost crude oil or washed out its hold, they cannot, for a distance of miles, stop and find food because, as they swoop down, they find only oil beneath them. And one by one, they see their companions dive in and drown because they couldn't manage to fly up again.

With genuine insanity, humanity condemns to death the creatures around ourselves. In the last century, humanity has destroyed hundreds of species, that have been literally erased from the earth, and which had taken millions of years to evolve!

And let's speak about our pets, too. Let's take the simplest example: that of the dog. We know that a dog has a shorter life than that of a human being, it lives approximately fifteen years. For this reason, if we are given a dog as a present when we are children, it will die before we become an adult. It is an experience that so many of us have had.

Many people deal with the problem of their pet's dying by having it put down with an injection, but it is not, except in unusual cases, a good thing. Many times, instead, a dog is left to die alone. This provokes a genuine trauma in the animal that, having always lived in the home, psychologically feels as a part of the family.

A dog who lives in a home is not a dog but a person, who does not realizes they are walking on four legs instead of two. It tends to copy its master, especially if it has been brought up with a child; it too would like to come to the table, and sleep in a bed or behave as it sees the others doing. It is taken aback if it is not allowed to do so.

It feels certain it has the same rights, because it sees itself as one of the family. Then, at the moment of death, this air of affection that has been building up around it throughout the years, is suddenly broken. It sees strange behavior on the part of those people who, only a little while before, showed it so much love, when it was able to run and play. It finds itself left on its mat, neglected and ignored, right at the time when it most needs affection.

The same treatment is reserved for some old people. Everything is fine for as long as they have their wits and are entertaining; then, when they begin to be a burden and a nuisance, we notice they dirty things, they smell, and all the inconveniences come out.

It is always and only a question of selfishness. We hide behind false pity: "But he is suffering... Let's see him die rather than see him suffer..."

To cry inconsolably for someone who has died is the saddest of things; it means binding the dead person to matter with your thoughts.

The widow who mourns her deceased husband for ten years does him harm, she keeps him trapped in his astral body, she stops him from casting it off easily; she chains him and makes him suffer. It is therefore not an act of love to be upset for a long time and constantly keep alive in grief the memory of someone who has died before us, but an act of great egoism: "I hold onto your memory, I cling to it and I preserve you in my mind."

Now that you know, if you find yourself in the situation of mourning someone for years, let go in your mind; let them go on their way, and do not make them suffer solely for your egoistic desire to hold onto them.

You will be reunited when something greater than yourself decides on it. Remember with joy, and not with grief, those who have crossed the threshold before you.

When the heart stops beating and the body shuts down, death has not yet come about: several hours have still to go by before the perceptual abilities cease completely.

Very often, you can still feel with your body for as many as eight hours after the cessation of cardiac activity. I refer to the case of someone dying in their own bed.

You are still in your body and, if you are not prepared for it, during those hours you will try and let the others know you are still alive. You would like to move a finger, a hand, give some sign, but you can't manage it. You would like to cry out: "I am still alive," but you cannot. The person who is aware and prepared for what is happening, can utilize this time much better, can make use of it, that is, to get ready for the next stage, for really dying.

It is not a case of resignation but rather understanding what is your own death. Someone who dies without understanding their own death, prepares for a poor life; above all, for the next life, they are launching themselves from a poor springboard, revealing that they have understood little of what they have lived through up to that moment.

Fear, during death, comes from this: wanting to communicate with the outside world and not being able to do so. Once beyond this phase, fear no longer exists; there is no pain, but only the sensation of floating. By becoming good at out-of-body experiences, you will get through this phase very easily.

In the moments following physical death, after ten/twenty minutes, you are able to perceive the concerns of the people around you, and you can almost hear their thoughts.

Their true, honest thoughts come in this moment, and the things they hid for a whole lifetime are revealed, synchronistically[6], through that terrible divine humor!

And so it can happen, that you can hear friends and relatives, you thought were close and affectionate, rejoice in your death, out of jealousy or motives of self-interest.

6. Synchronicity refers to the possibility of interacting with events, beyond the laws of cause and effect.

And then, whoever has just died might ask themselves: "Did I really deserve this treatment, or are the others bad in thinking these things of me?" Of course, the opposite can happen too, that is, you can discover feelings in people that you never even suspected.

From this point of view, we can imagine the death of powerful people. How many think: "At last he has gone!"

And how many schemers, who took advantage, hiding behind the person of power, to further their own interests, say to themselves: "What would have happened if he had not died? Perhaps, sooner or later he would have taken me out, for everything I've done against him." And it turns out, possibly, that that person was kept alive in that body not out of love, but only from political motivations, forcing him or her to put on an appearance of life, which is really terrible.

Certainly, for some reason, from a karmic point of view, this person deserved such a treatment, given that they got it; but, according to the same logic, whoever delivered it will experience it in their turn. We always deserve what comes to us: never anything more nor anything less. That does not mean that life is stingy with us; on the contrary, at every opportunity, it offers us the best fruits; it is up to us to gather them in time, and nourish ourselves on them, taking care not to let them go rotten. What counts most of all is to always have the courage of one's actions, without being influenced by others' choices and without trying to influence those of the next person.

In certain moments, having the power to do so, in a fit of rage, who of us wouldn't have liked to hit someone, even someone dear to us? If we were all in the habit of following our instincts in every situation, and if we had the possibility of impose them on others, what would happen?

A Wise Man once pondered this, "We are in the habit of naming our kings when they are still children.

# LIVES XIX

*What has been has been*
*you cannot change the past*
*but the future*
*is already marked*
*and I'm living it*
*in the eternal moment*
*as it happens*
*until the nothingness*
*when I shall think no more.*

And we say that, as the king is all powerful, it is right that he can always express all his desires! It then happens that the old king dies; he has a four-year old son. This four-year old child becomes king.

Then, all his wishes, all his games, his whims become law; and there is the risk that no one will be left on earth, because the day the king drops its beautiful glass ball, and it smashes into pieces, he will want to kill the whole world. Of course, his glass ball is broken, and all the world must perish for this!"

It is a fixed rule: in certain moments, we are capable of anything. Even if—and this is a fixed rule—often others think we want to do something worse than what we really have the intention of doing.

# And we come to the moment of death...

And we come to the moment of death. When we notice we are about to die, it will be of great help to concentrate on the color sky blue[7]. It is very important to fill the mind with positive, calm thoughts, perhaps saying good-bye and thinking of good wishes for the people we are leaving behind. We succeed in dying well when we have learned to die thinking not of ourselves but of others. So long as we continue thinking about ourselves, about what we are doing, about what is happening, we are not helping ourselves at all.

7. Sky blue is the color of relaxation. Imagining oneself enclosed in a sky blue wave thus helps to loosen tension, to relax. It is a good rule, each evening, before going to sleep, to breathe deeply for a few minutes, imagining a sky blue wave coloring every part of our body. Such an exercise will help get rid of tensions accumulated during the day, and will make sleep deeper and more refreshing.

During death, we rejoice in great bursts of light; it is important to really enjoy them, with all our being: we will gain a lot of incarnations, because we will have grasped a moment of eternity.

My invitation is to put everything into it, because we shall not be given a second chance: even when death comes again it will not be the same.

It can also help to weave a sky blue cocoon around yourself. To do that, you should wrap a blue wave around your body, by imagining a thread of this color winding around your body, as if you were weaving a real cocoon. In this way, you shall be protected from every kind of interference that could disturb this moment, which is yours and yours alone.

It would be really good if each of us went to sleep at night ready to die. "If I were to die this night, would I be ready? Or would I be leaving things still to be done, or things half done?" If you ask yourself this question every evening, to begin with the reply will always be:

"No." Later on, you will notice you are little by little better prepared, and this will be a personal conquest. If you like, you can call it "the evening prayer."

At any moment you should be able to say: "Here I am, my friends, I am ready... I stand at attention... I just have to go on my way, whatever that might be, in whatever moment..."

The vision of death that each person has, is conditioned by the idea of death that has been conveyed to them. For the sole reason that, at the moment of death, everyone relives his or her own life, a person will be their own judge, and cannot help but be an objective judge, even against their own will. Thus they will know, on the basis of the moral principles they were taught, if the actions taken were good or bad.

They will find themselves before paradise or hell, as they have always imagined them. Obviously, the soul has nothing to do with all this and it will take its own road. But the part of us that is an astral double will have the experience that the person expects.

Thus, whoever has imagined a catholic paradise, will experience that; whoever has imagined a paradise full of houris will experience that. Materialists, instead, who consider death as the end of everything, will reach their paradise in the annulment of every sensation and need.

At this point, you could think of getting up to all sorts in life, to enjoy things as much as possible, hoping to save yourself at the last, on the basis of a game of convictions. And yet, not only the name of whomever does it will be cursed as long as their memory remains, but if they have wasted a life, they may even turn back in the chain of reincarnations. And it will make no difference whether they believe it or not.

Here we go: it is your turn. In this moment, it is you who are dying. And while you are watching a really fast movie of your life flashing before your eyes, the others too, all those are around you, are living, each in their own way, this same adventure.

The phrase: "When I die, the world dies with me" is only pure selfishness. Just think that, in this moment, the state of your consciousness, the way you are feeling, is something you have already experienced other times because your soul is eternal and remembers. What is happening has happened before and will again in other circumstances, in other moments and —why not?—in other spaces, probably. So then, why worry so much about this death? Accept it as it is, as it comes.

53

I am convinced that there is always a touch of envy, if we can look within ourselves, with regard to the person who is dying. So then, the situation of the dying person is not as bad as is generally thought. And the first to realize that this is not a bad state is precisely you who are dying. After all, you would also like to leave a good impression. In fact, you think: "It's true, up to now I haven't done so much: at least, I can die well. I'll put all I've got into it, and see what I'm capable of doing."

When you are about to die—and you realize it—listen to some music. If you like it and it is "yours," when you listen to it, its notes will turn into a ladder, your ladder, safe and precious. Upon it, it will be easier for you to leave your body, and go up. I have already said I remember several past lives and how many times death has been a faithful companion to me. But now I can tell you that the most peaceful of my deaths was miraculously accompanied by the sound of a guitar, I still remember the sweetest of notes!

Every moment, every situation, every experience has enriched you. Now, dying, you must not throw out the window all those precious things. What you have lived through is permanently a part of yourself, of your "me," in this garment and in this time.

The more you have known how to live well and with intensity, the more your spirit will be alive. This life of yours—any life at all—is a sieve which, through very different experiences, refines your being.

Have no fear of dying, you will be able to take all of yourself with you.

And at a certain stage, once you have reached the right vibration, a luminous point will appear above you... it will keep on expanding... pulsating as it gets bigger... it will become the portal through which you will pass.

We must realize that no one of us is indispensable, not even for our own children. It is only a form of presumption and egoism to think of dedicating all our lives to our children. No one of us is indispensable, and so important to be absolutely remembered, even if everyone is convinced of the opposite. Some time after our death, apart from the grief of those left behind, everything of us passes away. All there is left is an idea: everybody prefers to remember us as we were when alive.

If we were indispensable, we would be eternal! And, indeed, we are, but from another point of view. Besides, everyone must live their own life and let others live theirs.

Life belongs only and exclusively to the individual, and to no other.

All this would have no value if life did not have a purpose, which is to participate in the growth of something greater, an organism in which each of us represents a cell which must exist to have its own experiences.

We can compare humanity to a tree which, from being a sapling, has to grow. We may be a healthy part, or a sick part of the tree. It does not matter. Sooner or later, all the leaves will fall because there is always an autumn; but in spring new buds will bloom, perhaps right where before there was a leaf.

Is it possible then to plan for one's own death? Firstly, it is important to live well. Often, one lives with a dissipated spirit, completely lost in work, preoccupied only with tomorrow, thinking: "I can buy a car in a year's time, and a house after that..." Or else, sighing: "Lord, let me live at least until my children are grown up, so that I can help them." And again: "Lord, grant me enough life to see my children sorted out with work, married... see to it that I get to see my grandchildren walk!" And this can go on, of course, forever. Often, I sense people thinking these things.

If these are the only things for which we live, at the moment of death we will find ourselves without any past, without having lived, therefore unworthy of dying. So death is transformed into an unpleasant, tragic event. Some, for example, die screaming they don't want to die, shouting, cursing everyone. This is not, undoubtedly, the best way to die. It would be nice, instead, if we could all reach that moment with a smile on our lips, with peace of mind and simplicity, prepared for a unique and non repeatable event.

Remember: a way of helping ourselves is by starting to help others, perhaps, respecting the death of others as if it were our own. Or else, on a more down to earth level, putting in order those things that matter

# LIVES XX

*The only satisfaction*
*is the bitter awareness*
*of the instant*
*I have just lived*
*and the drawing near*
*of the last moment.*
*Then I shall no longer be able to worry*
*nor shall I be able to understand*
*why I shall no longer exist.*

most to us, making a will, leaving in writing our last wishes, our last choices, in order not to be concerned, at the moment of passing, by things left unattended.

To plan for one's own death also means asking questions like these: "What will remain of me, afterwards? What can I do with what I have? If I were to die tonight, weighing the balance between what I have done and what I could have done, how would it be? What are the things I should have done, and those I would have liked to have done... and what have I done instead? ..."

Think of yourself a minute ago: it is easy to see that your "you" of a minute ago no longer exists. If you are now, you are no longer a minute ago. The same argument can be applied to the self of five minutes or twenty minutes ago. In this time, everyone has built something new inside of themselves: each one of us is the result of what we build upon ourselves.

We always think about ourselves with reference to the past, never to the future: if this does not restrict us, it can be right, in that beyond our eternal present—when we are aware of it—we are also what we have built upon ourselves. No instant lived can be reproduced by any other human being, it is unique and, as such, has an enormous value and a nobility; and we need to learn to live it, and to go through it.

It is well to ponder this every now and then. A moment ago, while I was thinking up these sentences, I was so very convinced of living that moment of my existence; while now, I can see myself of a moment ago, from outside, living that moment, by now gone and not repeatable.

Was that moment ago lived intensely? Was it lived as it deserved? Or was it a completely anonymous moment in the flow of time, and nothing more? Before dying I will review all my life as if it were a very fast movie, and I will relive this moment.

Therefore, I will be here, thinking about my death. And I will remember having reflected on it, I will remember what I am saying in this precise moment.

If I have learned something now, this something will be useful then!

You can have a little chat with yourself who is dying, along the lines of the following: "Do you remember when you read all those interesting things about death in that book? Well then, now you are in the moment in which you are living them. Thus, this is the time to see if you lived well, if you are prepared, if you put into practice what you read."

So, to avoid the panic that overcomes so many, let's try and follow all those suggestions that we are reading now, and that, at the crucial moment, will pass before our eyes again, allowing us to relive them moment by moment, as we will relive all the events of our lives: from the insignificant events—like that fall at three years of age—to the bigger things, like the first time we made love.

Each one of those past events will be a present moment lived as we live our death, in that precise instant.

So let's carefully prepare, starting right now, the topic of our death because, for certain, we will go over these moments. Let's try to learn these suggestions as much as possible, so that we can use them at the end of our movie. At the end of a film, there is always something which makes a reference to the principal theme, to what the plot was about. I repeat it again: if you do not learn to live well, to live every moment in the most intense manner, it is useless talking about knowing how to die.

To live well, from another point of view, can mean living according to one's own ideas, without being influenced by others, in any circumstance or situation. To live one's own life, in whatever historical moment, making sure that nothing influences us— except in extraordinary circumstances.

Or, if there must be an influence, it should be us, who choose it. The choice of an Initiation, for example, presumes a life spent having chosen your own influences. But it is, indeed, a choice. It is like a seed, which decides to sprout in one type of soil rather than another.

Whoever chooses like this, it is because they have had a reason for it, and their reason is synchronistic.

Our state of consciousness is a way of feeling things, living in situations, which varies from moment to moment. When we get out of the wrong side of bed in the morning, we have a certain type of consciousness, which leads us to evaluate our problems according to that particular state of mind. Thus, our evaluation of the way things are varies all the time, in relation to our state of consciousness.

It is very important to remember that we are always in an eternal present, and the evaluation of our "me" is strictly conditioned by the state of consciousness of the moment.

Therefore, in the moment in which we die, we risk being bound to what was our last eternal present.

Managing to live our now well, creating calm, pleasant states of mind for ourselves, we can prepare for a good death.

It is like doing a bit of cleaning at home: it might only be a little, but nevertheless it contributes in tidying up and dusting the chair you are going to be sitting on.

When a person dies, they die physically to be reborn in another life. They are reborn in a way that actually parallels the physical: thus, they have to learn once again to take their first steps. This will come easier, the more rapidly they managed to detach themselves from the physical body. In this case, they can be helped, in addition to their own preparation, by meeting other already dead people who, therefore, know what to do. This is an opportunity as rare as it is beautiful. The physical presence of other people who are able to send thoughts of love is also important.

This too is something very beautiful, that all of us can do with ease.

For the self to completely separate from the body takes seventy days, which are extremely delicate. They are the hardest, most difficult days to get through;

it is the time that nature concedes to a being that dies, to detach completely from the physical sheath and get ready walk along a new path. Above all they are difficult days for whoever is not prepared for it, as remaining attached to a body that is rapidly decomposing, without knowing what to do, is not pleasant. The most fortunate have friends close by, who can help them get through this period.

There are some tribes who, to help their dead, burn their bodies and eat their ashes. There are peoples who consider the moment of death a great celebration and they are right, because it is the opportunity to take a step forward.

Some can remember their past deaths and this can be of some help. I say some because, at the crucial moment, emotion can play nasty jokes, just as can concerns about the life just lived, for, in these moments—as I have already said several times—we see everything like in a movie.

When we die, we stop using a body; we take off one garment to put on another one, which allows us to have new, different experiences. And we will continue to incarnate until we have understood several fundamental rules: we are not indispensable; we have to live our own life.

You can die in many ways and for different reasons; let's take a look at a few possible kinds of death.

You are at the wheel of your car, going home or to the cinema, perhaps wrapped up in some problem about work. Suddenly, two headlights appear in front to you; you are so taken by surprise that you do not have time to react. It's an accident: the car crashes. From that moment, your sense of perception operates in slow motion: you see events as extremely slow. You do not feel any pain; you do not even have an idea of pain. You do not realize what has happened. Your mind, with its attachment to life, refuses to accept it.

All of a sudden, all the sounds disappear, everything moves extremely slowly, even though your body has been thrown from the driving seat, and flung far away. Every second becomes a month, a year. Suddenly, you can see again, like in a movie that runs at an enormous speed, the whole of your life; you see it again as if you were reliving it in that precise moment. Your attachment to life has the effect of prolonging it for you.

In those moments, your self is outside of you, and looks at your physical body: it notices every detail, nothing escapes its attention. It is as if the barriers between conscious and unconscious were gone, allowing you to take in everything with enormous clarity. Only afterwards, when you have relived all your life, and the car keeps on rolling over, do you realize what is likely happening. "What is happening to me? It's impossible it's really happening to me! It can't happen to me." This is the first thought that strikes you in such predicaments; it is not an idea you will get out of books or that you will hear going around, however it is an experience that happens to everyone.

At times, these kinds of events, can be sensed a few moments before they actually happen or, even, can be a punishment that we inflict upon ourselves.

A lot of accidents happen precisely for this reason: often death is not by chance but—as we have already said—it is a case of unconscious suicide. It is the wish to die in that certain manner and moment which turns into a reality and, if we decide to have an accident, this happens exactly as our unconscious has planned it.

So, we have a slowing down of the sequences, the disappearance of sounds and noises which return only in a few cases: past emotions, the alarm clock, the office, the dentist, the moments when bad things happened to us; the whole movie of our life, with a spontaneous evaluation of the good and bad we have done.

These are the things that pass before our eyes. There would be so many beautiful things to remember, if only we could appreciate them. The trouble is that often we are not capable of giving value to our life. How many times do we behave like automatons? What we earn we spend on nourishing the body and not the spirit, in our leisure time we go dancing, to the cinema, and then we start all over again: sleep, work, make some money...

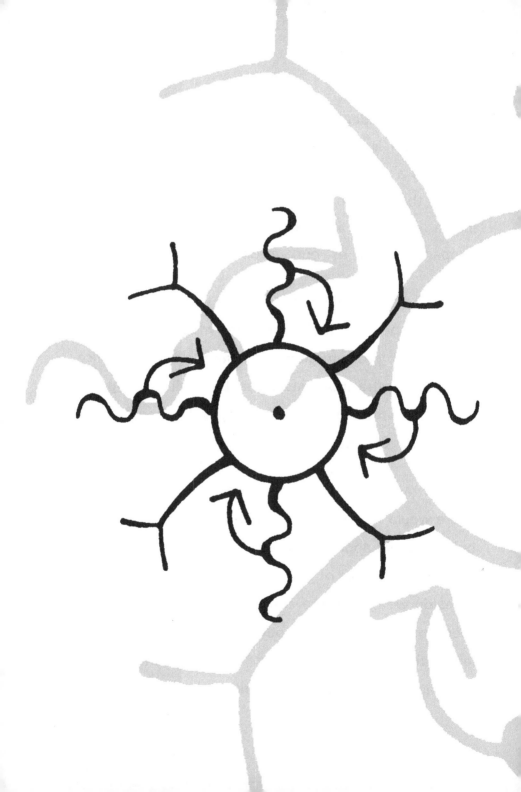

## ME 2.

*And who am I?*
*What am I?*
*What do I exist for?*
*What am I looking for?*
*Whoever can answer me*
*will have discovered*
*what life is.*

Let's go back to the accident. Let's suppose that death occurs. In that moment, you feel literally ripped out of your body and you find yourself, all of a sudden, outside of it, but still tied in some way, to your physical body. Above all, you find you are unprepared. In that moment, all your thoughts are focused on the events that are happening. And you do not realize you are dead! On the contrary, you might be convinced you are not hurt at all, while instead your body is mangled.

At that point, you get up from the ground, you smooth down your clothes and you approach the crowd of curious onlookers gathering round to savor the accident. Addressing them, just to reassure them, you say: "Thank goodness, I'm not hurt."And they don't even reply, as if they hadn't heard you. You touch them, then, and it is as if you touched nothing. At the most, whoever is touched might have the impression of a cold breath on the back of their neck, or of being brushed by an insect. But you still do not realize you are dead.

Let's suppose, you decide to return home. You have the impression of walking, of going down the road on foot but, in reality, nobody can see you. You arrive home, go up the staircase, ring the bell noiselessly and somehow manage to go in: but nobody notices you. Perhaps, those still at home do not yet know of your death, or else have only just found out. But they do not see you, they do not hear you because, for them, you lost your life at the place of the accident[8].

Things, then, get complicated, as the days go by. 73 Little by little, you begin to become aware of something, like a cord, that gradually becomes less elastic, rather it tightens and pulls you beside your physical body, until you notice you can no longer go very far away, because you are held fast beside your corpse. Sometimes, you are even forced, by this link, to go back into your body; this however depends on what kind of preparation you have in relation to death. The cord slackens only if you have help.

8. Falco tells of a similar incident, that he witnessed in person when he was a boy, in his book "Tales of an Alchemist," Niatel 2012.

It can happen, at times, even just with the last rites, as long as the officiating person has a certain ability and believes in it—a necessary condition for any rite to really be of help. From the moment of death—as I have already said above—around seventy days go by, before you can completely detach from your physical body.

Another possibility I want to examine is death from illness, at an early age. Our example: a person of thirty years of age complains of headaches; he goes to the doctor, they do a dozen x-rays, his pain turnes into a tumor. Thus, this person has only a few months left to live. How does someone behave, when they find out? Do they have sufficient maturity to accept this fact, or do they feel as if they've only just started living in that moment?

In the second case, feelings of rage and desperation might arise. They might decide to go around town carrying a knife, to leave their memory behind at all costs, no matter if it is stuck in someone else's side. Far more often than you can imagine, this is a thought that crosses the mind of those in this condition.

But there is also the person who is a little calmer, who reasons more or less thus: "All right, I have a few months left to live... I can believe it, or not believe it... however I will try to live my life, just as I have always done up to now. And then what happens, happens!" It is a stance of calm state of mind.

I advise whoever happens to find themselves in this situation, to evaluate their life with a kind of examination of consciousness, and to undertake to live well at least what time is left.

To live the last months in a way that they acquire the value of at least thirty years. Because it is not true that dying at thirty years of age is a waste of life.

Certainly, generally, one is at the height of one's powers; and, often, one is living the fullest and most beautiful period. Then, there is nothing else to do other than keep on living the present with the same intensity and learn —if one has never done so before—to prepare oneself. It can be an opportunity to meditate and to be ready for what will happen, trying to overcome fear, developing detachment, planning well everything that will happen.

To die well does not mean letting yourself die at the first opportunity, straight away giving up the fight. I am not saying you have to invoke death to free yourself from your suffering. To die well means also struggling to live, but with dignity, courage and in silence: to die without making a fuss, because death is a private, precious blessing.

Let's look now at another kind of death: let's think of the person who dies of old age. Usually, they die more alone than the others, because by now they are no longer productive, they are a nuisance, are of no use, and are only a burden. Sometimes, unfortunately, when an old person dies, their loved ones breathe a sigh of relief. "God, set my father's life free, from this suffering, he is old by now..."

It is a powerful thought, which is justified as freeing from pain; while, in reality, it is those remaining behind who wish to be freed from an old and useless being.

Today we have completely lost the idea of the wise old person, rich in experience. In its place we have that of the rich old person with pots of money who, in the eyes of their heirs, seems mean and attached to their wealth, which they would like to get hold of as soon as possible.

I am of the opinion that, by continuing to live a pace of wake up-go to work-have dinner-go to bed, when we get old, we will not be rich in experience at all. On the contrary, we shall be rich in so much stupidity. This way then, we really will be useless beings. If we do not do something about it, the fate we shall earn for ourselves will be euthanasia[9]. What we inflict on others, one day will be turned against us. How can we hope to be accepted by our children, when our turn comes, if today we treat our parents in this manner?

9. Falco repeatedly stated that everyone has the right to a dignified death, and therefore, ultimately, to request euthanasia. However, it is important that this is the conscious choice of the individual, not of those - such as relatives and healthcare workers - who are around during the person's last days of life.

.

# ATOMIC WAR

*The first one has gone off:*
*horror of trembling hands;*
*the second one thundered:*
*a wagon of rags*
*is what remains*
*of men.*
*With the third*
*was the last scream;*
*the fourth:*
*the grain will ripen no more.*

If you see to it that someone has a bad death, you will be repaid in the same coin and you will have that death. Not only, but you must know that, in the period we are living, which is at the beginning of the Age of Aquarius[10], this kind of reckoning is meant to be settled immediately, not left over for the next incarnation.

Suicide is another type of death. You must bear in mind that death from violent causes does not happen again, if it was an experience that was lived intensely; if, on the other hand, it was lived badly, or was not reflected upon, it is possible that it might be repeated.

A person who commits suicide encounters a great many more difficulties, precisely because, usually, they are not at all prepared for death. This happens to those who escape into suicide, that is, when they are unable to accept life.

---

10. Astrology divides history into periods lasting approximately 2,000 years each, called "ages", based on the of the precession of the Equinoxes. We are now in the beginning of the Age of Aquarius, a time of spiritual awakening. The Age of Aquarius will bring great changes also on a social level.

To know how to die it is essential to have learned how to live. Killing oneself means not being able to face life; at times accepting it requires a lot more courage than seeking death.

After all, it is not so difficult to seek death! Thoughts of suicide go through everyone's head, in as much as they are part of what we all must evaluate, for the sake of experience. We weigh up the possibility of doing something like this, even if this does not mean we have to do it.

A very different matter, on the other hand, is the suicide of someone capable of understanding the lives of others. This could be called "initiated suicide". It happens when a person offers their own life to save that of others.

When a child dies everything is easier. Usually, if a child dies shortly after birth, it is because that being still had to have that type of experience; it was missing, so to speak, that step to be able to go forward. This step forward comes about through birth and a sudden death.

That is, it is a case of a compensatory birth. When a child dies a few days before birth, it is something else still, as the body did not yet host any consciousness.

The problems relative to the death of a young child are a lot less serious, because it is a very free spirit, in that it is much less bound to all the things that would have happened consequently, determined by the upbringing, their way of thinking, and so on. We must remember that a child is instinctive, hence it acts instinctively. The memories and experiences it makes use of will be those of its closest past life. And since the last experience it went through was its death, it will manage perfectly well.

A child a few months old can wake up one morning recalling, all of a sudden, dying "a little while ago" in a battle at sea, or having loved music, and so on. Many cases of child prodigies are a demonstration of very effective links with a past life.

Not only that, but since a child is a clean and pure spirit, usually, its death is often fairly quick, and very often the seventy day rule does not apply. This is true for children who have not yet reached a certain age, and thus have not yet formed a personality, which is around four-five years. When, however, a child has already acquired a personality of their own, things are a little different, as it has already developed a very definite way of thinking.

I should like to refer briefly to two other kinds of death, that due to nuclear explosion and the phenomenon of apparent death.

Whoever dies in a nuclear explosion receives damage not only, as is obvious, to their physical body, but also to another one of their subtle bodies. This will have inescapable consequences for their successive incarnations.

I refer to the bodies, of course, and not to the soul, even though it too, while simply by reflection, can show some signs of a set back.

Statistics and surveys from around the world report many cases a year of people thought to be dead, who subsequently awake in their tombs. The legislation of each country requires a minimum number of hours that must elapse between presumed death and burial. Certainly, however, it would be much better if, besides the doctor, there was also a psychic present to confirm if it is really a case of death. They could advise if it would be better to wait a little, thereby avoiding a terrible experience for those unlucky enough to find themselves in that situation. In a few countries, precautions in this regard exist, like that of slipping a needle into the brain; indeed, a lot of people ask for such a proof for fear of waking up buried alive.

Death is almost always accompanied by fear, which may be summarized into three main types.

The first type is fear of death itself, because one does not know what it is; another is fear of the suffering, which is thought to accompany death, and this is perhaps the greatest fear. What usually gets to us is fear of physical harm, more than that of death.

The fear of death is only a consequence of the fear of the pain of death.

The third kind is fear of death, out of nothing but fear. It is the fear of being afraid, and cannot be overlooked because it creates a powerful negative expectation. It is very similar to the most common fear in humanity. The majority of people who get healed are really sick with fear: fear of pain, fear of living on, fear of death, because if I die who knows what might happen... and so on.

Well then, they are all useless fears, because whoever dies is forgotten by everyone, after the emotion of the first while, and has to go on their way alone. As is only right. Everyone lives their life which is neither more negligible nor more important than that of any other. Therefore, from this point of view, whether it is a great Head of State or the lowest poor wretch who dies, there is no difference: the relation with the death of the first and that of the second is always the same, albeit their passing has hugely different repercussions.

The death of an individual who has left their mark on an age, is still only a death; and it is but an istant they have left their mark upon.

When that moment is gone, the situation will be completely different; it is useless building great tombs for famous people, the following generations will only use them for tourists.

Often, our mind connects death with pain, while death is never suffering and pain is, in reality, fear of pain. Nobody suffers during death; it is as if, after a long journey through the desert, we were to find ourselves, suddenly, at an oasis, so that there is an overwhelming feeling of peace and relaxation, a feeling that makes you think: "At last!"

Only at that point do we realize that the element in which we were moving before was definitely not our own: it was a useful element, perhaps, for the experience it gave us but, all in all, not worthy of us. The less you are stained with the earth, the less you are "stained by humanity," the more easily you can succeed in grasping and making this idea your own.

It is the moment of passage, the most important moment of your existence: it is a really beautiful thing because it is the passage to the true dimension of the human being.

I repeat: a sense of peace and calm, no pain. In that moment, everyone is alone with themselves and sees, at last, a glimpse of what divinity can be, the "thing" they will go towards afterwards.

In the moment we turn the page of a book, for a second it catches the light: dying is like turning a page, in that moment we perceive a flash of light.

At the moment of death, everyone is alone with themselves, while their senses begin to fade one by one, until the hearing goes, which is always the last. In the end, only you remain, for you did not live only in relation to what you wanted others to think of you. Now, all of everyone's talk, their opinions of you are only dry leaves swept away by events. The tree trunk remains, which is you. A little winter.

It is important, every now and then, to be alone with oneself for a while. I recommend doing this spiritual exercise from time to time.

Instead of the usual wasted holidays, harassed by the crowds and the radios, moving from the heat of the city to that of the beach, try, for example, to remain in your apartment. Lower the blinds and spend a few moments in peace, centered in yourself, to meditate.

Moments like these are supply stations for the train of life, which goes on, and on, and, at a certain point, stops at a little station to rest a while, to take a break, to assess what has been achieved up to that time. Without worrying about specific details: what matters is learning to be alone with yourself and to "feel yourself," lying down on the bed, with arms and legs a little apart, as for astral travel, and practicing breathing slowly and deeply.

It can happen that, for the first time in your life, you learn to listen to your own body, to notice how it is made;

you discover you have a pair of feet, each one of which has five toes, with a little toe and a big toe and you realize you never thought about them before, except when they were hurting. You might even discover a mole on your right side: since it is part of you, it is a good thing to know it is there, to be aware of it. This simple exercise, this contemplation of yourself, helps you be aware of existing, helps you be aware of living now.

And then, think about death; about those you leave behind, about the things you still need to do, about oblivion... In such a way, you will begin to feel confident with it, to talk to it. And it will become a friend of yours.

To plan for your death can be a thought that initially brings a lump in your throat. But a mature person must be able to do it, even for the sake of others. It would be well, therefore, to deal with the really practical aspects, from sorting out how things will be divided among your children, so that each one has his or her share, to taking out—why not?—an insurance policy on your life, in order not to leave your family with problems.

# GRATITUDE

*Great men*
*of times gone by*
*one thing you should know*
*fill up with indignation*
*for your monuments*
*are of use only*
*for the pigeons.*

Planning is also a way of exorcizing your own death. These are also, in their way, rites for a good death. And I hope no one is shocked just by this.

It is surely difficult for a doctor to say to a patient: "You have two months of life left, then that's it."

And it is even more difficult to hear it, without going crazy. We can react with disbelief, or even with despair. Or we can accept it, without starting, from that moment, to behave strangely: "Oh, is that how it is? All right then... I'll have to die anyway, sooner or later, it doesn't make much difference. At least I'll do my best to die in the best possible way."

The situation is often complicated also for your relatives, who know how serious your illness is, but do not dare talk to you about it. If they are informed before you, they might even question your ability to accept the news without making a drama of it. This is, indeed, an extremely delicate problem.

You might notice that their attitude towards you changes... and you begin to suspect something.

After a few check ups and as many clinical tests, that give you clear guarantees that there is nothing wrong with you, absolutely nothing at all, you realize the family around is becoming affectionate, attentive as they have never been before.

Also your relatives, including those you haven't seen for at least twenty years, visit you with eyes swollen from crying... At this point, you realize what the situation is really like: "But then... I am not going to last for much longer here..." At times, as a consequence of this, the mind of the sick person starts playing strange games, for example, that of jealousy: "After I am dead, what will my wife do? Will she get married again or not? I don't want her to marry again..." This is a bizzare form of jealousy, arising in precisely these situations; it is a way of feeling caused by the constantly changing states of mind.

And anyone who has lots of boring relatives, or with a pinch of humor, might think: "At last I will get rid of so many unpleasant people!"

Tranquillity, in relation to death, depends also on your family context. If your relatives have some sort of spiritual preparation, for sure there will be the necessary strength to face this passage together that can really be a great joy.

In ancient times, some peoples used to have days of celebration for death. When it was known that someone would die, they were told; indeed, some people even made an announcement themselves. Of course, among those peoples, every individual was prepared; they made provision for this preparation from childhood. Thus, the person about to die got ready as if for a celebration; they said goodbye to all their relatives because they would be going on a long journey: "I am going away... I greet all of you... Probably we will see each other again... What have I left to do? The wishes I have left, I will try to make them come true now.

The most important thing, however, is to live this solemn time with full awareness, because this is my magic moment..."

Death is like a baptism: dying well leads us to the right road. Life can be compared to a banquet: you arrive, you take your place among the other diners already present, and you begin your meal. You eat a starter: your youth; you eat the main course.

Sometimes, there isn't a main course, or else you don't make it to the coffee or the ice cream, because you have to get up from the table. At times you stay to the end. There is always the moment in which you have to get up, say goodbye to all those you have met at that banquet and go on your way. Just as, one by one, the other guests will also go on theirs.

"Here we are, I have finished eating, I have to stand up and leave. First, I will have to say goodbye to the people next to me, who shared this meal with me. We have a good time together and I hope I made a positive impression on them."

There are also those who want to leave their mark at all costs so, they begin to pour the wine, laughing shamelessly. All they achieve is to spoil everybody's meal. In turn, they will have bad indigestion. Death, indeed, is the moment of digestion; it is the time in which you process what you ate at lunch and you see the outcome.

The results can be of three types: you ate too much and haphazardly, and so you throw up, thus wasting what you ate at lunch. Or else, you ate adequately and digest it well; you had a good meal and therefore you can move on, you get ready to go to sleep in expectation of getting up the next day to start a new life, to nourish yourself with new food that will make your soul and your experience grow. The third kind of result is that of someone who got themselves into the worst situation. They were neither fish nor fowl, that is, they chose the middle of the road, not committing themselves one way or the other.

You may become a great saint, or a great bastard that is better than living in the middle of a lukewarm road.

The saint teaches the others how to sit at the table; the bastard leaves a mark that makes others ponder their own values.

Those who live in the middle of the road, that is in mediocrity, do not achieve anything, not even for themself. They waste their lives because the relations they set up with others are totally wrong. They live neither to be of help to others, not to be cool: they are only a faded, mediocre, sorry figure. They delude themselves they are eating at the table of kings, while they actually find themselves at the table of the swines.

To live well means living your own moment, knowing and understanding in depth your own role and remembering the esoteric rule: "Aim high." If you aim low, you will miss the target; if you aim high, your arrow will land in the sun. The aim of life, in the light of my experience, is Knowledge, in as much as God is Knowledge; hence, to search for God, through Knowledge, is the purpose of life.

The Knowledge of God passes through various faces, that is the different aspects of the truth: the truth, in fact, is a crystal with infinite facets, of which we see only the one we are able to see, or the face we are allowed to see. Our task is to manage to consider the greatest number of facets possible.

I suggest you to consider life like a sonata for the piano, where rhythms and movements follow on from one another in a harmonic whole, studied in all its components. A good part of humankind views life, instead, as banging out notes on the piano, that is as a succession of accidental notes caused by changing, fleeting emotions, aims and deeds that have nothing to do with the pursuit of Knowledge or even the dignity of humankind. This is not the way to live. We should choose our every moment, every "now," and live it intensely, rather than planning our lives, which means living tomorrow.

It is interesting to note how so many people are afraid not so much of death, as of the presence of the dead:

they are not prepared and thus they do not understand death. The dead person is not dangerous, they are not someone who can do harm, rather someone who should be helped. I once watched a significant scene: they brought a woman who had fainted to the hospital; the nurses lifted her from the stretcher to put her on a couch.

Owing to the effect of muscular relaxation which happens in those particular circumstances, the woman wet herself and so wet a nurse; he didn't bat an eyelid: "Poor woman, these things happen." After about fifteen minutes, there came the news that the woman had died; the nurse looked at his shirt, which was still wet and exclaimed: "How disgusting!" All because the woman had died, rather than fainted.

The fruit of our ideas and our actions are genetically passed on to our children, and by them to our grandchildren. When they reach a certain age they will give expression to what they have inherited from their parents.

# TOMBS

*A slab of sky*
*will be the cover of my tomb*
*the spirals of earth*
*the walls, the wind will bring me*
*the darkness will be my light*
*the boundless and nothingness*
*my land*
*and no longer shall I know*
*above and below,*
*breadth and depth,*
*but I shall be at the centre*
*and everywhere*
*and nowhere.*

I am not referring only to what the parents have been purely up to the moment of conception; the son or daughter will continue to take from their parents for as long as the latter live, because the children will continue to be united by a bond which we can define as telepathic. And their parents will have an influence on them not only through their example, but also throught their genetic heritage.

It is a little like what happens with the children of drug addicts, whose newborn babies have to be given valium to calm the withdrawal symptoms. However, another type of drug, the drug of life, is passed on to our children and to all of the people close to them. We always influence the life of whoever is close to us, and our children in particular. By living well, we will pass on this attitude and our children will live well, and their offspring too.

It is not something terrible to let a child see a dead person; on the contrary, it is a fine thing, because a child will not be frightened, providing we don't do our best to frighten them! This way, children get used to death, and very often it can be they who help the deceased person.

In some countries, there is even the custom of having children kiss the dead, and it is really a good thing. Which, however, becomes really horrible if the parents show that they are disgusted, and all the same force the little one to kiss the dead person, in this way causing the child a definite trauma.

Let's learn something else of great importance: to reflect on our life. To live continually reconsider-ing the way we live; to live with a good accompaniment on the piano, with a base rhythm that has some merit. And thus we will play much more bountiful scores. It is one thing playing a funeral dirge with long, deep, very frequently repetitive notes. It is quite something else to play a minuet, which is a real piece of embroidery upon our lives. Too often we forget these opportunities, also because the others, perhaps without meaning to, do everything to ruin our harmonies. If we live our life in this way, in a more intense manner, every instant with a greater presence, we realize that the lives of an unemployed person, of a professional, of a Head of State, have the same, identical worth.

After death, we get ready for a new incarnation. We will face death once again, thus learning something new, something useful for our own evolution. In some cases, it is useful to know, consciously, the reason why we have reincarnated; in others, it is not.

How does reincarnation happen? In some cases it is very quick. Let's take for example a road accident. After the crash, you leave your body, make all those attempts we talked about earlier to be noticed, then you black out.

And, a moment later, you open your eyes again; you feel a slap on your bottom, you hear your voice which is that of a newborn baby, your body feels warm once again. How much time has gone by? Out of surprise, out of shock, you suddenly forget what happened earlier. Not always, however, is our return so quick; in many cases, waiting for a new body is much longer.

Let's dwell a moment on the indifference with which, we think about the death of others. When it is a case of someone else, especially if we do not have any link of affection with whoever has died, we tend not to be interested.

So long as death has nothing to do with us, it is a matter only for others. Each one of us regards ourselves as eternal, until we start dying. But since we start dying the very same moment we are born, let's not give ourselves any illusions: life, if you like, is nothing other than one long process of dying. It is up to us to make it pleasant or at least dignified!

The first rite of a good death, which everyone can always put into practice, is that of using thought well. Let's imagine we are faced with the death of someone dear to us: what shall we do? Let's think about it while this person is still alive. Our husband or wife, our parents, our sons or daughters, our dear friends... Generally, we turn away from such thoughts; we want to avoid the trauma, the despair and all the bad things that go with it. However, these events sometimes happen when we are least expecting it, when we are least prepared for it. Thinking of their death is not a case of negative thought; on the contrary, it can even become a thought that avoids the drama, a thought that acts as a lucky charm.

If you plan your death preparing for it as it were the most important event in your life, also all those around you will have this same disposition.

The funeral should not be an exhibition of grief and crying, but a peaceful walk, which accompanies the deceased person to where he or she—or rather, their physical body—will rest for a certain number of years.

It can happen that someone gifted with particularly well developed psychic sensitivity, may find themselves, when following a funeral procession, side by side with the dead person, chatting with them. And when they come across someone with a sense of humor, they can hear comments of this kind: "Well, well... we're off for a little walk... Let's have a little look at who's at my funeral. See here, so and so is missing, he didn't even show up. But, look, she is there! I did not expect to see her, how nice!"

It is better to bury the deceased in the earth rather than in burial niches, in order that what is born of the earth, may return to the earth. The release of our being is quicker and more harmonious, when we are buried in the earth, as the frequencies[11] are more compatible. Better still if the coffin is thin and not made of zinc, in order that the body can follow the normal process of disintegration. It is absurd to want to preserve one's body at all costs, and it is even harmful, since the more rapidly the body disintegrates, the more rapidly we free ourselves. However, it is important that we leave clear instructions, so that whatever solution we choose, it is the result of a conscious choice[12].

11. "Frequency" refers to a concept similar to that of the radio. It is the compatibility of someone with something, or of something with something else. If, for example, you want to listen to a specific channel, you have to tune into the exact frequency; otherwise, the sound will be indistinct and there will be interference. Here Falco refers to the compatibility of our physical body with the element of earth.

12. In recent years, Falco's advice became that of being cremated, as cremation allows the energies connected to the physical body to detach more easily. Falco made this choice for himself.

At one time, it was the custom to put all the objects belonging to the deceased in their tomb. This happened in times when objects were much more expensive than now. In spite of that, people were buried with all the jewels, weapons, and equipment they possessed.

Those things bound the deceased to this life and it was therefore appropriate that they were placed in the tomb. Now, on the contrary, we prefer to divide between the heirs even the last of the rings.

108

Today this custom has disappeared, also because, in the past, so many tombs were desecrated by thieves; but it really would be a good custom to put a part of the belongings dear to the deceased in the tomb, as this would help the person during their first seventy days after death. If we do not do it today, it is only out of greed and ignorance. The more respect there is for death and the more an object of value—even if only of sentimental value—linked with the dead, should be left with them in their tomb.

On the contrary, it is essential to avoid putting things belonging to others in the coffin, even less photos and belongings of living people. It is however ok to place in the coffin objects belonging to people who died a long time before the deceased, to whom he or she was particularly attached.

# A speech to someone who is dieing

I want to finish this text by speaking directly to you who are reading this: this book was written for you, to help you live your death well—please excuse the play on words,—and to help you prepare for the death of those close to you.

Try and identify with the scene I describe: the person who only a moment ago, as they looked at you, still showed signs of life, has lowered their head exhaling the last breath of this existence. You are taken by surprise: you did not imagine this moment would come so soon, and that you would be there to witness it. You feel awkward, you think you do not know how to behave, what to say...

However, you know now that you can be of very great help to the person who, in this moment, is starting a long journey. It is not at all true that everything is already concluded. In this moment, it is as if the dead person has only bought the ticket for the train. He or she is waiting for it to arrive, will have to get on it and do a great many other things.

Precisely in these circumstances, you can be of help to them. I can suggest a plan, which you can follow in your own way.

Above all, remember to keep the lights low: the brightness of the lights creates a pressure on the body, which makes it difficult to leave it.

Then, get all outsiders out of the room. Move close to the bed, breathe deeply a couple of times, trying to empty your mind of all thoughts not relevant in this situation. Then speak to the dead person in this way:

"Now, you find yourself in a new, completely new situation, different from that of a few moments ago. Now, you have only just started living, that is, you have begun living a completely new life. So, listen to what I have to say to be of assistance to you. I hope, that when my turn comes to take this step, you will be at my side to help me in the passage.

Above all, you are not suffering. I know that you feel well; you find yourself in a situation of great peace, you are relaxed and you feel well. Try to relax, to let yourself calmly leave your body. Don't strain to give any signs since, in any case, you can't make them reach me. Even though your eyes are closed, your hands are not moving, and you can't speak, I know you are listening to me. Let yourself go, because this is your moment. Let everything happen quite normally because, until you are ready for the long journey that is awaiting you, your train won't come. There are people, not far from here, who are in despair, who are crying: don't let yourself be bound by the weight of their emotions, don't get emotional because of them. Even if they are screaming, think only of living this moment in the most intense way. This instant is all yours, it is the most important moment of your life.

You have lived a certain number of years; you have done many things and you have had your experiences. Now you are getting ready to have new ones. Try, therefore, to start well, by getting on the train which is about to arrive with dignity and calm.

Be ready for it! And, of course, you can stay close to us in thought, because we don't want to forget you. However, think that you are about to become part of something that is much greater, and this is the most important thing!

The end of your life is only the end of this life. You'll see, there will be even more important and interesting lives for you. Perhaps, a much more adventurous life is awaiting you. And it may even be that in a while, in the next life or in a few lifetimes, we will meet again.

In this moment, you are drawing very rapidly closer to God.

Perhaps, reflecting again on what you did during your life, thinking about what happened to you, you are realizing that some things you did well, others not. And you are preparing your self-judgement. Maybe, you can be at peace with yourself. The things I'm telling you are for this specific purpose: to make you feel at peace.

It's the only help I can give you, because I'm not yet very well prepared to talk to you about these things. However, I can assure you that, if you keep calm, if you manage to let yourself go, and leave with ease, it will be possible to move on. Not only, but you will also be able to prepare a better path for us, who are going to follow you."

This is the gist of what you can say, or read, to someone who has just died. All the rest, the details, you'll find them within yourself. They must come from your relationship to him or her.

Perhaps, only in this very particular moment, you'll manage to say what you never dared say before to that person. Perhaps, you can get it together to say: "I love you!" If you never said it before, if you didn't dare, because your pride was in the way, because it wasn't that kind of relationship, you can manage to do it now, because emotion is pressing you; because the person who is dying is entering into a different state to you; because he or she is moving away from you.

This is the time to start saying all those things you never managed to say in so many years of friendship, or living together. Perhaps, it is your time to get to know yourself better, with whoever is dying. All the rest, if you look well, you'll find within yourself.

Well, our little chat has come to an end. I hope these notes can be of use to you; meditate on them, it will not be a waste of time.

Every now and then, re-read at random a few pages of this book, you'll find you can discover something new every time. I could have changed these pages into something more learned and elegant. I didn't want to. I believe that simplicity and explaining the way I think in a straightforward manner, can, more easily, create a communion not with me, but of you with yourself.

And, if I may say so, "Good Death, Brother and Sister!"

*On June 23, 2013, Falco leaves his physical body. In one of his last meetings with the Damanhurians—smiling in spite of his obvious suffering—, he says farewell to all with these words, "Love each other, love each other, love each other. Being close to each other, you will find the solution of love, forgiveness and comfort. What I ask of you is a love that everything comprehends. The love of which we are a part. I greet you with love."*

# DAMANHUR, FEDERATION OF COMMUNITIES

Damanhur, is an eco-society based on ethical and spiritual values, awarded by an agency of the United Nations as a model for a sustainable future.

Founded in 1975, by Falco Tarassaco (Oberto Airaudi, 1950-2013), the Federation has about 1,000 citizens and extends several hundred hectares of territory throughout Valchiusella and the Alto Canavese area in Italy, at the foothills of the Piedmont Alps.

Damanhur offers courses and events all year round, and it is possible to visit for short periods as well as longer stays for study, vacation or regeneration.

Damanhur promotes a culture of peace and equitable development through solidarity, volunteerism, respect for the environment, art, and social and political engagements. Damanhur has a Constitution, a complementary currency system, a daily newspaper, a magazine, art studios, a center for research and practice of medicine and science, an open university, and schools for children through middle school.

The Federation of Damanhur is also known throughout the world because its citizens have created the Temples of Humankind, an extraordinary underground work of art dedicated to the reawakening of the divine essence in every human being. It is considered by many as the "Eighth Wonder of the World."

The art studios that made the Temples are located at Damanhur Crea, a center for innovation, wellness and research, open to the public every day of the year. Damanhur has centers and activities in Italy, Europe, Japan and the United States and collaborates with international organizations engaged in the social, civic and spiritual development of the planet.

120

Via Pramarzo n. 3 - 10080 Baldissero C.se (TO) - Italy –
Tel. +39 0124 512236
www.damanhur.org

# Index

Lightning Source UK Ltd.
Milton Keynes UK
UKOW06f0843210715

255554UK00003B/24/P